Thunder in the Valley

The Massabielle Saga

Since the first candles faintly flickered and glowed, and fervent aves echoed o'er the swiftly flowing waters of the Gave, Mary's wish has lovingly swelled into a tremendous crescendo.

The castellated rock of Lourdes reverberates the prayerful praises of thousands upon thousands of her children, as holy **"Thunder in the Valley."**

Thunder in the Valley

The Massabielle Saga

by
Rev. James H. Klein

ST. PAUL EDITIONS

WITH ECCLESIASTICAL APPROBATION
Archdiocese of St. Louis, MO

ISBN   0-8198-7316-0 cloth
        0-8198-7317-9 paper

Printed in U.S.A. by the Daughters of St. Paul
50 St. Paul's Ave., Boston, MA 02130

The Daughters of St. Paul are an international congregation of
religious women serving the Church with the communications media.

CONTENTS

"Lourdes is a Divine oasis of Faith, Hope and Love in a desert of human suffering." *Verily* a place."where faith reigns and God is alive."

With deep appreciation I wish to acknowledge many sources from which I have gleaned names, dates and historical data to make this story as authentic as possible. In some instances poetic license was employed without detriment to the veracity of the events portrayed.

His Holiness—Pope Paul VI
Cardinal John Wright
Bishop David Maloney
Monsignor Novarese
Father Donald Wuerl
Mr. and Mrs. Wm. Barry
Gene Kramer *
Holy Scripture
William Shakespeare
"The Pope Through the Ages" Rev. Jos. Brush-ers, S.J.
"Lives of the Saints" A. Butler

numerous magazine articles and periodicals.

Dedication

To my dear brother Raymond and sister Florence. Their great love for our Blessed Lady was most inspiring.

May Mary the Immaculate Queen of Heaven welcome them to Eternal Happiness in the Kingdom of Her Divine Son....

Prologue

Father James Klein and I have become dear friends because of our association at Lourdes. We have concelebrated, with hundreds of Priests, Masses at which tens of thousands received Communion in the manner cherished by our people in Boston, St. Louis and all over America.

We are on our way to meet Christ, Whom we meet in His Church, His Saints, His "little ones." Thanks to Christ we shall one day face God, but for that we must pass through the door of death. These realities are very much on our minds in Lourdes, despite many false conceptions concerning Lourdes. One is that it is a place of tourism: it is not. It is a place of prayer. Another is the shallow talk about the "Commercialization of Lourdes." That is largely nonsense. Millions of people come here every year, and I for one always want a cup of coffee or a roll and perhaps some medals for friends and relatives. If I have the right to buy these things, then so do millions of others. So there *have* to be stores, and stores mean commerce, if you want to call it that.

But in the great park of the so-called "Domain of the Grotto," there is no touch of the business of this world. Wherever you look you see the suffering, the paralyzed, sometimes the almost literally dying, but you see them smiling and praying. Their smiles are the smiles of people whose souls are perfectly at ease and at peace. It is the chief place in the world where you see people wait for hours on their sickbeds and in their cripple chairs, grateful for the slightest kind deed, word or attention. How do you explain this? The explanation is very simple. They know the secret, the secret of life. The secret of life and the joy of the joyful Christian are both to be found in the cross. Lourdes is not a place of profit or sight-seeing; it is a place of Hope...Faith, Hope and Charity.

Lourdes is a place of joy, beauty, gentleness, sweetness, peace. The Shrine, the cloistered park around it, the countryside, the processions, the candles, the music, all speak to us of happiness, but none of the people who come as Pilgrims to Lourdes is deceived by any mere air of tranquillity, joy and beauty. Each one knows that all of these things are consolations, to be sure, but that they come from the Cross. The Cross is the Key that opens Heaven. It is the secret of how even the most desolate, abandoned and unhappy can be made joyful who learn, in the words of that old song "The Rosary," "to kiss the Cross."

Joy in the Cross was preached by St. Paul and is present at Lourdes. It is the whole point of the life and death of Christ, as it must be of the Christian. At Lourdes one finds it in the sick, in the Stations of the Cross, in the monumental crucifixes that are

16

found everywhere in this holy place—placed on every path and hill as if to keep us from becoming too sentimental about the mere consolations of the Christian life, or too "Romantic" about the songs and folklore surrounding the true place of the Blessed Mother in our lives. Remember, the same woman, the Mother of Christ, who is the Cause of our Joy, is also the Mother of Sorrows, even as the Christ, who is the cause of our Salvation, is also the Example of the Suffering we must welcome if we are to die and rise again with Him. This is the heart of our faith, of our hope and of our love.

Nowadays we talk much about love; not a little is sentimentality, "enthusiasm," even error. Love consists in self-giving, even suffering and renouncement. All love must not be self-interest or self-centered but in the service of life and of man's *Love* built in the laws of God.

There is no life that is not touched with suffering, and if all you have to offer is "good cheer," then, if you are a priest, you are going to lose the spirit, and if you are a layman you will lose the point. The priesthood is a life of suffering, in the shadow of the Cross, but always with the hope of Heaven. So in the case of a marriage if "love" is all there is, then "When love goes out the window the marriage is finished." What becomes of the marriage of those who suddenly find that one of the spouses has an inoperable cancer and is faced with years of suffering? It is then that the greater love begins, not *ends*, because love is always compassionate service of those whom we love.

For example, when Father Klein and I first came to Lourdes we came on a train with about five or six hundred Italians, Americans, Yugoslavians and others. Had we asked them what love is, above all, love of the Faith, we would have promptly learned that the Cross stands in the center of true love for Christ, His Church and all else. On the train we distributed crosses to remind the people that there might be cures, to be sure, and there would certainly be graces, most certainly those of joy in anticipation of the joy of Heaven itself, but only thanks to the presence of the Cross at Lourdes and in our lives—that Cross which is the Key that opens Heaven to us all.

J. Cand. Wright

John Cardinal Wright

Chapter One

The Secret of Pain and Grief

"The Massabielle Saga" is presented fervently hoping to increase devotion to our Blessed Mother —to better understand in some small way the tremendous part she can and does play in our daily life—if only we ask, if only we pray.

Every man's life contains the elements of joy and sorrow, and may be divided in three parts: Past, Present and Future.

The Past, shrouded in memory, is a garden in which we walk the path of yesteryear and view at our leisure, with joy (or displeasure) the fruits of precious time, now fled to eternity.

19

The Future, wrapped in a cloak of uncertainty, is fraught with nebulous dreams and ambitions.

The Present is the *now* wherein we live and breathe, experience joy and happiness, pain and sorrow. Happiness we seek, love and cherish; pain we fear and fail to comprehend.

Pain is a purely subjective experience. The crucible in which God tempers the spirit and purges the alloy and dross of fallen nature. Pain can emanate from many sources, such as the inability to cope with problems. Worry may generate tremendous mental anguish and grief. Disease, a deterioration of the body, can produce excruciating agony. Medical manuals list thousands and thousands of maladies and malfunctions that rack the human anatomy.

The sorely afflicted children of hapless Eve ever seek the bridge that spans the chasm between torture and hopeful peace and relief.

A merciful Creator grants man relief in many ways: He has given the knowledge and scientific skill to cure many ills through medicine. When and where these are, at times, inept—Divine Providence miraculously intervenes through the media of prayerful devotion to the saints, especially Mary, His Immaculate Mother.

When things are right and life runs smoothly, man has a tendency to bask in the sunshine of a pacificatory euphoria. Tragedy in another's life is given polite sympathetic understanding. In a blissful state of innocuous desuetude man's prayers become routine, without ardor, often, mere poll-parrot repetition of pious words.

Media Center

United Nations

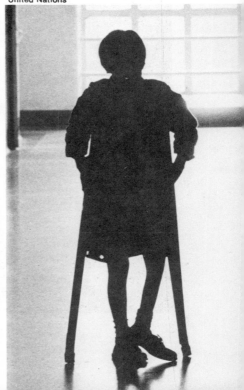

But let tragedy strike—and the doctors' diagnosis is that the illness is "incurable, terminal, crippled for life," and there is "no hope—no hope as far as medical science is concerned," then in pain the fervor of his prayers becomes most passionately intense. He storms the gates of Heaven; God listens as he pours forth his heart and soul in agony.

> "But they say the tongues of dying men *enforce* attention like deep harmony. Where words are *scarce*, they are seldom *spent* in vain—for *they* breathe *truth* that breathe their words in pain."
>
> Richard II (Shakespeare)

The thieves crucified with Christ spoke words in pain; one blasphemed, the other prayed, "Lord, remember me when You shall come into Your Kingdom"—"This day you shall be with me in Paradise." He had looked into the dying eyes of Jesus and had seen a king.

There may be times in life when deep depression may cloak the heart and mind of an individual

23

rendering them irrational. In complete despair, they may even contemplate self-destruction or some other obnoxious act. If only these misfortunate souls but look into the heart of Christ crucified, they will see that "the cross He permits is of wood and cannot last. The crown He promises is of glory and cannot be taken from Him or from those to whom He gives it. Good Friday was for a day. Easter is forever. Worry in the hearts of the devout is the darkness of a single night. The courage of a Christian is the dawn of a day which has no end."

—John Cardinal Wright

Calvary must be relived in every soul until all shall have made their peace with Christ. Standing on the Via Dolorosa in old Jerusalem, I thought—

"I saw the Son of Man go by
crowned with the crown of thorn—
was it not finished, Lord, I said,
and all the anguish borne?
He turned on me His awesome eyes—
'Hast thou not understood? Lo;
every soul is *Calvary* and every sin a rood.'
And by that sight
I saw the light—
thus did my grief
for Him beget relief,
so learn this rule from me—
pity thou Him and He will pity thee."
(69, "I Knew God By His Pain")
John Cardinal Wright

Crocellà

"Now there stood by the cross of Jesus his mother." "I read that she stood," says St. Ambrose; "I read nowhere that she wept." Yet tears there doubtless were—silent tears, noble tears, tears like those of Christ whose co-sufferer she was.

The measure of Mary's grief is the measure of her love as she gazed on the flesh of her flesh, mangled beyond a mother's power to heal. When, therefore, Jesus had seen His mother He said, "Woman, behold your Son"—and to His beloved disciple, "Behold your mother." Thus, God entrusted us to the care of His loving mother, so she may aid us in our need—in physical, mental and spiritual sickness.

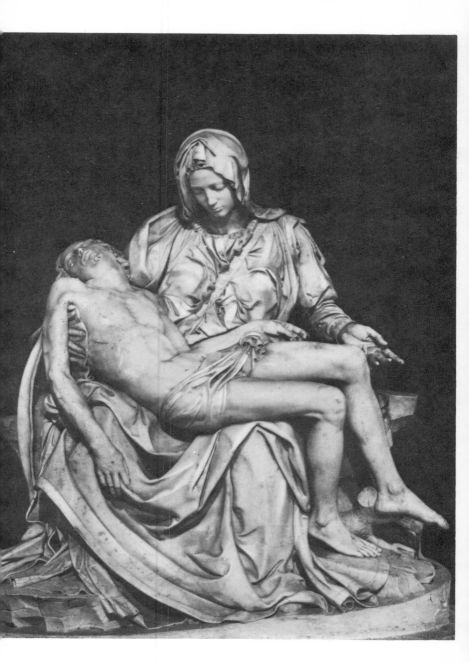

27

The devotion of the faithful throughout the world has chosen Mary "Health of the Sick"—healer of bodily ailments and help of those in pain—as "Consolation of the Afflicted." She teaches the proper value of the crosses God sends man, and never to despair of His Divine Help.

Mary has appeared on many occasions to Holy Souls in diverse places. The most famous apparition possibly is Lourdes—known as the "Pain Capital of the World." From the four corners of the world an army of grief-stricken, suffering humanity wends its tortuous way to this small village—tucked away in the Pyrenees Mountains of Southern France. All are seeking the help and consolation that the world was unable to give, each fervently hoping for divine intervention through the intercession of Mary, Mother of God.

Chapter
Two

The
Apparition

The beautiful story of the apparition in the Grotto of Massabielle, near the confluence of the Savy Brook and the Gave River, is a story of the deep love God's Mother has for her children. Bernadette Soubirous, small of stature, frail, suffering from chronic asthma, at age 14 years, was granted the singular privilege of seeing and speaking with Our Blessed Lady, and of conveying her message to the village people and to the world. François and Louise Soubirous, the poorest of the poor, had the dubious privilege of living in the *cachot*—an abandoned jail considered unfit for vagabonds and evil-

The Soubirous Mill.

**The paternal home
of Bernadette.**

doers. Four children shared one room with them, freezing in winter, roasting in summer. Two barred windows looked out on the yard that was the dunghill of the whole neighborhood, stinking to "high heaven."

François Soubirous supported his family as best he could by performing odd jobs. Louise made a few *sous* by working on occasion for the more affluent ladies of the village.

One cold raw day, Bernadette with her sister Marie and a schoolmate, Jeanne, on a wood-gathering mission chose the vicinity of Massabielle to accomplish their chore.

The Apparition. *(Painting at Rome.)*

The Grotto in 1858.

Bernadette, due to her physical frailty, remained on the tongue of land between the brook and river, opposite the cavern in the chalky cliff—a place not favored by the people of Lourdes or the peasants of the nearby villages. Massabielle was just a cave, bare, damp, filled with rubble of the Gave floods. Old wives' tales were many, of dread and ghostly happenings on this scene. Jeanne and Marie crossed the brook to gather the wood. Unable to follow, Bernadette suddenly became aware of a beautiful lady standing in a pointed niche in the rock in the cavern. She was clothed in a snow-white garment much like a bride's. Wavy ringlets of light brown hair escaped under the veil. A broad blue sash, lightly knotted under the breast, fell down over the knees. Her tiny narrow feet had two golden roses placed above the slender toes of each foot.

Bernadette's whole being, so overwhelmed by the spiritual, radiant beauty, was transfixed. Trying to bless herself, she was powerless. The Lady raised her right hand and slowly made a great, gleaming Sign of the Cross, and the child was then able to do so in turn. The Lady nodded and smiled approval. Bernadette raised her small black Rosary. In the hand of the Lady appeared a gleaming pearl Rosary with a radiant gold crucifix that reached almost to the ground. Bernadette told her beads ever so slowly. At the end of each Ave the Lady let a pearl glide through her fingers. Marie and Jeanne, returning with a great mass of fallen branches, were frightened at finding Bernadette pale as a corpse, Rosary in hand and kneeling in a rigid, curious posture. They rudely aroused her— the beautiful Lady was no longer there—but there remained a blissful feeling within the frail little girl. On the way home, Bernadette revealed her experience to the other girls, exacting a promise from them not to tell anyone, begging them to restrain her from returning immediately to Massabielle. Somehow she knew the beautiful Lady would be waiting for her.

Hardly had the children returned home when Marie broke her promise and told her mother of

Bernadette's experience. Louise Soubirous, frayed by the day's frustrations, lost her self-control. She accused her children of being worthless gadabouts propagating nonsensical stories. She grasped a flexible cane and the first blows fell across Bernadette's back. The younger children did not escape her anger. François, awakened from his nap, joined his wife in berating the youngsters. Shortly after this domestic scene things changed for the better. Relatives and friends began to appear at the door of the *cachot* bringing gifts of food and good will— even with a job for Soubirous himself.

The amazing events of the Eleventh of February, 1858, soon spread throughout the whole area. Bernadette's mother sought counsel of one of the parish priests concerning the eerie happenings. She was informed that they were harmless phenomena of childhood with which mature people need not bother their heads—that settled the matter. Accordingly, on Sunday when Bernadette, surrounded by a crowd of school girls, begged permission to take her friends to visit the beautiful Lady of Massabielle, permission was reluctantly granted.

The Lady was not perturbed by the presence of the other girls. This time Bernadette was not the distance of the width of the brook from the Lady, but so near that she could almost touch her. The girls had brought a vial of holy water along and Bernadette sprinkled some in the direction of the niche saying: "If you are of God, Madame, will you please come nearer?" Smiling, the Lady did come forward to the edge of her rocky oval.

Photograph of Bernadette.

The Soubirous Family.

Despite the antics of the girls, Bernadette was entranced. Frightened, the children sought help and the owner of the Savy mill came and carried her to his home. Her rapture had ended. Louise Soubirous was enraged when called to the scene and had to be restrained from striking her daughter. Fearing for her health, she made her promise never to go to Massabielle again. "I promise, unless you yourself give permission." Later the miller and his mother discussed the situation of the Soubirous and decided that no good would come from all this.

The happenings at Massabielle grew in dimension. The tempo of interest accelerated and conjecture ran rampant—What? Who? Why?—were the main questions on the tips of wagging tongues. Doubting atheistic pseudo-intellectuals rejected the possibility of preternatural or supernatural happenings at the cavern. The whole thing was just a scheme to gain attention—the figment of the imagination of a young, silly girl. There were some who dabbled in metaphysics with a pert interest in ghosts and spirits. Such a one cajoled Louise into allowing Bernadette to return to the cave and ask the Lady if she were her dead niece. Accordingly with lighted candle, the first to burn at Massabielle, the disturbed woman had Bernadette ask the Lady the question. The Lady shook her head and laughed. Then after Bernadette took out her Rosary and prayed, the Lady spoke for the first time:

"Will you render me the grace of coming here each day for fifteen days? I cannot make you happy in this world, only in the next."

A crowd had gathered by now. They questioned Bernadette, and she told them of the Lady's re-

quest. Some promised to make the pilgrimage daily
with her to the grotto, feeling that they would learn
many truths from this favored child. When they returned to the town more than a hundred excited
people gathered. Some jeered—some believed—the
policeman feared a violation of the law of the
Regime of Emperor Napoleon III, who had himself
come to power through street riots, knew the power
of, and thus feared the mob. Another crisis arose in
the Soubirous family. Louise and François were
prevailed upon by Louise's sister to stand by Bernadette, and even to go with her to Massabielle for fifteen days.

Early next morning several hundred people gathered for the trip to the grotto. Many carried lighted candles. Bernadette flew like a swallow, like a leaf in the wind. The Lady's benevolence was more intense as though through the fulfillment of her wish, an important and far-reaching plan was beginning to be realized. Now there were many in the crowd who were prepared to believe in the presence of the Lady in the grotto. There were a few mockers and many just curious. A woman began the first Ave of prayer; others joined, making a thunderous chorus of many voices. Suddenly Bernadette arose, and seeing her mother's desperate face she threw her arms about her. Then many wept.

The local café was a clearing house for the crackpot unbelievers whose erudition increased noticeably by the glassful. The Mayor was asked to render a report concerning the breaches of peace at Lourdes. Local civil authority was at a loss of how to handle the affair. The Church, in the person of the Dean of Lourdes, refused to become involved in the turmoil, instructing the local clergy not to set foot in the grotto and to ignore the whole matter.

Bernadette was subjected to a third-degree type of questioning by the police. Next morning in school a nun held her up for ridicule before the whole class. That afternoon Bernadette, mysteriously restrained from returning to school, was inspired to go to the grotto. The local gendarmes followed her. The Lady did not appear.

On the morning after this tragic happening Bernadette was granted an incomparable reunion with the Lady. The crowd started to chant a hymn of praise to Mary. A man began to poke a stick into the niche. Bernadette screamed that he hurt the Lady. The crowd forcibly removed him from the grotto. The Lady told Bernadette to go to the priests and tell them, "A chapel was to be built here and let processions come hither." Although frightened, Bernadette obediently conveyed the message to the Dean of Lourdes whose irascibility was loosed upon the terrified child: "Tell the Lady to perform a miracle by letting the wild rose that grows in the grotto bloom now, at winter's end."

Chapter Three

Go to the Spring—
Drink and Wash

The whole town buzzed with the Dean's message to the Lady. The liberals and anti-clericals looked upon this demand as a juicy joke.

On the very next day Bernadette delivered the Dean's impertinent message to the Lady. Again and again the word "Penitence—penitence—penitence." Bernadette responded by kissing the earth and crawling on her hands and knees until they bled. She tried to incite the crowd to imitate her penitential acts, but with little success—they had expected a miracle of the rose—there was none. The Lady soon withdrew.

40

The next day, Thursday the 25th of February, was regarded by the miracle-hungry as the testing day. An estimated five thousand souls thronged the chalet isle and the gendarmes roped off the grotto. Only Bernadette and her relatives and closest friends were allowed inside the lines.

This day Bernadette found the Lady solemn, rather stern and restrained. Beckoning the child closer she ordered her to go to the spring and drink and wash. There was no spring, so she started towards the Gave, but the Lady called her back, repeated the order concerning the spring, and as though to help her, she added, "Eat of the plants there." In the far corner of the grotto a few blades of grass and bitter herbs grew. Bernadette crawled over to them and ate. There was no spring, so she clawed into the earth. Some water began to appear, moistening the earth. Taking the Lady's words literally the child washed her face with the mud and then swallowed some. Nauseated, she vomited. Her mother and relatives brought water from the stream and cleaned her face and hands. Bernadette was too feeble even to observe that the Lady had abandoned her.

The spectators thought that what they beheld was a repulsive aspect of mental derangement— was this to be their miracle? The mass of humanity laughed, not so much at the child, but at *themselves*, for their stupidity and easy credulity. The crowd dispersed slowly, wagging their heads as only the wise do, having been duped by the unwise —finding it not so easy to get over disappointment and disgrace. Some who witnessed the Crucifixion of Christ *also* wagged their heads, unable to comprehend anything beyond the bloody, mangled body hanging on a cross. "Vaugh!" was their expression of contempt used to show disappointment.

The majority of Bernadette's followers were sad and reproachful. The unbelievers gloated openly. A crowd gathered at the cachot. François asserted his fatherly prerogative by showing the relatives and erstwhile friends the door, telling them not to overcrowd his home again.

One of those ejected was a partially blind stonemason who had an uncommon idea—returning to his own home, he had his small daughter obtain some of the moist earth from the spring. Making a poultice of it he placed it on the ailing eye. After a period of time he removed the pack. He was staggered by excessive light and was able to see the outlines of things with precision. He raced to the doctor's office shouting, "I can see—it's a miracle!" When asked if he could read the letters on an optical chart he said, "No, because I don't know how to read." Medical science was unsure whether this case came under ophthalmology or psychiatry.

Bernadette, totally absorbed by her visions, was indifferent to public approval. On the next morning only a few people gathered at Massabielle. Bernadette knelt facing the niche and took out her Rosary and prayed. The Lady was not there. Some women burst into tears when told. A change of attitude took place—there was no longer any doubt about the girl's sincerity.

Later that afternoon the stonemason went to get some fresh earth for his eye at the grotto and discovered a few women looking at a thin trickle of water running from where Bernadette had clawed in the earth. "We were telling our beads," they said, "when the water suddenly began to run." "As God lives, that's spring water!" cried the stonemason. With the help of some fellow craftsmen, working at night by torchlight, they built a basin to hold the water that by now was flowing in a stream of the thickness of a child's arm. All the workmen drank greedily of the spring. Bernadette was given the wonderful news only when the work was finished.

The formation of the spring of Massabielle added impetus to the controversy. The apparitions became an affair of broadest import. The Bishop of Tarbes admitted the possibility of the supernatural; thus, he must exercise the utmost caution. The civil authority, as expected, acted in the usual wise and decisive manner: the Soubirous were put under strict supervision—especially in respect of money received for the unauthorized sale of consecrated objects, blessings, etc.

On the next day Bernadette was persuaded to use a neighbor's beautiful coral Rosary instead of her own little black Rosary. Accordingly, when the salutations were over Bernadette produced the coral beads—but the Lady noticed and said, "That is not your rosary," and drew back as though hurt. "Where is your own?" Bernadette immediately took her black rosary from the neighbor and held it up for the Lady.

Chapter Four

Curious Travelers— Skullduggery

Curious travelers were beginning to seek out the Soubirous family—the strangers gazed at the paternal dwelling with mixed feelings of pity and astonishment at the wretchedness of this habitation. Some pressed coins into Father and Mother Soubirous' hands—these were accepted without false delicacy.

One day a man more genial than the casual visitor appeared at the *cachot*. Rather than look down on the miserable conditions of the place, he praised the orderliness. By saying this he won Louise and François' confidence. He then produced

The interior of the Soubirous home.

a flask of cognac and handed the master of the
house a beakerful. At last, the stranger offered to
buy Bernadette's rosary at any price. When this
was refused, he pleaded to have her bless his
daughter's rosary, but was promptly informed that
Bernadette was not a religious, didn't wear a stole,
and certainly could not consecrate anything.

45

The man then produced several large gold coins—"Would this be enough to buy your daughter's blessing?" The answer was a positive, "No." Undaunted, this stranger begged that his daughter's rosary be touched to some garment of Bernadette's —for this small favor he would pay handsomely. Louise took the rosary and thrust it under her daughter's pillow. Satisfied, the man took the rosary and then asked Soubirous to sign a receipt. Bernadette came into the house at this time, and upon perceiving the situation begged her parents not to accept the money, saying that the Lady would be angry if they did. François thereupon grandiosely refused the coins. The man angrily declared that a bargain was a bargain—arguing so long as he had the goods, Soubirous should take the money. He even offered to increase the amount. Soubirous refused, declaring they had no goods for sale. The man abruptly changed his attitude and with the cunning of a prestidigitator placed a coin on a bench, shook hands with François and took his leave. The only one to observe the coin was little Jean Marie who promptly slipped the glittering booty into his pocket—not for himself but to guard it from his family's dangerous idealism.

Media Center

Jean-Marie Soubirous

Marie Soubirous

The man was a stooge of the state; he had done his indecent assignment well. That afternoon on her way to school Bernadette was arrested. At the same time her parents were taken into custody and led through a whispering crowd to the provincial courthouse. The Imperial Prosecutor turned them over to the magistrate whose cherished aim was to prove Bernadette and her parents' specific guilt. However, the main purpose of this lamentable business was to paralyze Bernadette's visitation to the grotto on the next day—for rumor had it that something special was to happen and thousands were expected to be present.

The minion of the law roared and scowled, but the favored one of the beautiful Lady was calm. She denied accepting the gold coin. François and Louise also pleaded "not guilty." The Agent Provocateur proved to be a pitiful witness for the State. It was evident to everyone that the Soubirous had been tricked.

Upon questioning the children, little Jean Marie readily confessed he found the coin on the bench—Bernadette wrenched the gold piece from his hand and flung it at the government agent. The Judge put an end to the mockery by ordering them all out of the court. The Soubirous returned to the *cachot* escorted by a jubilant crowd. Some say that the stranger was handled roughly when he left town later that evening. He had served the State well, but not wisely.

The town's Mayor had grandiose plans for the spring at Massabielle. A facile pen could write the touching tale of a simple maid with a magic rod, guided by inner voices, striking the spring from the living rock. Lourdes would become a renowned watering place and his own financial status would be vastly improved. The Mayor's plans were not the same as those of Bernadette's beautiful Lady.

Chapter Five

First Miracle— "I Am the Immaculate Conception"

In a home close by the *cachot* some good women engaged in an ancient custom: the making of a shroud for a child about to depart this world. The doctor's diagnosis was that the baby, two years old, suffering from probable meningitis and polio-myelitis with complete paralysis of the legs, faced death within a matter of minutes or hours. Wild fancies beset the mind of the distraught mother —one image haunted her. The washing and dipping in the spring was no vain ceremony, but a purposeful mode of action which the Lady, through Bernadette, was constantly urging upon others. With a loud cry, the woman snatched the dying child from its crib, wrapped him in an apron and ran like mad to Massabielle. It was a race with death; a great throng of people joined the wild, macabre marathon.

On arrival at the spring, she immersed the baby up to its neck in the ice-cold water, stammering, "Oh Holy Virgin, accept him or give him back to me!"

Utter stillness ensued; even the death rattle in the child's throat was still. Then the thin squeak like that of a newborn infant was heard—the happy mother again wrapped the child in her apron, pressed it to her bosom and rushed back to her home. The baby slept for hours and upon awakening eagerly drank some milk and sat up in its crib for the first time in its life and laughed! Medical science was face-to-face with an unfathomable mystery—the first authentic miracle of Lourdes.

Thursday was to be the culmination of Bernadette's requested visits to the grotto. The cure of the moribund child would vastly increase the attendant crowd. All authorities were badly worried —maintenance of order would be a problem. It was decided to hold the military troops in readiness. The soldiers along with the gendarmes were to be in full parade dress. It would seem that the Lady for the first time had summoned to her ranks the French Army—the grotto of Massabielle was well guarded night and day.

From the hamlets of the Pyrenean peaks, from the villages of the ridges and valleys, a multitudinous hoard of humanity converged on Lourdes. At midnight they began to arrive, the aged whose alpenstocks shook in their trembling, palsied hands, joined the young and vigorous around the many campfires that blossomed in the valley of the Gave.

The moonless night was bitter cold. A few enterprising hucksters from Lourdes sold salami, cakes, brandy and wine. At the first light of dawn an estimated ten thousand had gathered. By the

time Bernadette arrived at the grotto, the crowd had grown in excess of twenty thousand. Their faith was no longer dependent on what would or would not happen that day—for what through the grace of heaven had been revealed to her eyes and the healing of the sick child was sufficient. For them, the Lady was there, and the usual ceremonies ensued—the eating of the herbs, the laving, the drinking of the water, the praying of the Rosary, the whispering, the salutations—half an hour saw the end of it all.

During all this the twenty-thousand peasants, plus the military and the gendarmes, were on their knees. Bernadette arose, her face radiant with bliss. The crowd broke into thundering applause. She was to return to Massabielle only when the Lady would let her know. When questioned if the Lady had a name, Bernadette revealed that she had said: "I am the Immaculate Conception."

The Church as yet had no representation at the grotto, but the Dean of Lourdes questioned Bernadette closely and was finally convinced—with reservations—that the girl indeed told the truth.

Demoniacal happenings increased round and about Massabielle as though all the forces of hell strove to discredit the heavenly happenings at the Grotto. Even François Soubirous fell from grace. Some men, unbelievers, tricked him by plying him with brandy until in a drunken fog he agreed that he indeed belonged to the "holy family."

The Prefect of the Pyrenees was directed to persuade the Bishop of Tarbes to effectuate a closing of the Grotto because of street urchins pretending to bless water and rosaries and loose women making fun of the Blessed Virgin. The Bishop thoughtfully fingered his jewelled pectoral cross. "You, Sir," he said, "only see the objectionable mischief, but in my diocese wholesome phenomena are being observed—prayers are more ardent than they have been in decades. Sorry, I cannot oblige you." Bishop Severe politely bade him farewell.

Bernadette was oblivious of all the conversations, speeches and interventions of the great of this world. On the eve of the last Thursday in March, she somehow was aware that the Lady wished her to visit the Grotto. The next morning Bernadette returned to the spring. Seemingly overwhelmed by her reunion with the Lady, she sank into a state of ecstasy deeper and more prolonged than ever before.

The usual rites, salutations and whisperings were almost wholly omitted. Only the praying of the Rosary was retained. Doctor Dozous, the municipal physician, had been present at the Grotto on other occasions, but this was the first time he witnessed Bernadette in a state of almost complete unconsciousness. She held her rosary in her left hand, a burning candle in the right. Slowly the taper sank down, so that the flame began to lick the outstretched fingers of the other hand. The doctor restrained the women from snatching the candle away. The flame quivered between the fragile fingers for ten minutes but the hand on examination was, except for a tinge of soot, unharmed. That afternoon the good physician reported these happenings to the Dean of Lourdes.

Chapter Six

A Decree—
The Shrine Closed

Having arrived at the conclusion that both
State and Church had failed, Mayor Adolph
Lacade, vested with the power to decide on all mat-
ters bearing directly on his community, issued a
decree. No one was to take water from the spring,
nor trespass on the property adjacent to Massabielle, and that a barrier of boards was to be erected
in front of the Grotto. The gendarmerie were to act
as watchmen. Violators would be prosecuted and
punished according to the letter of the law.

With stunning swiftness, a squad of workmen proceeded to put into execution the Mayor's proclamation. The collection box to gather money for the building of the chapel that the Lady desired, the votive candle offerings, the pictures of the Madonna, even the flowers, all were confiscated. A wooden fence was erected. Warning placards were put all around. Bernadette would no more be able to see the niche or the Lady from the other side of the brook. The next day at nightfall an infuriated crowd stormed the Grotto, tore down the scaffolding, and destroyed the placards.

Exacerbatingly slow, the ponderous investigative wheels of the Church began to turn. Bishop Bertrand Severe listened courteously to Dean Peyramale confess that he saw in Bernadette a true vessel of grace and that the cures of Massabielle were indubitable miracles. The Bishop broke in to remind him that Rome alone had the right to determine whether a given phenomenon is a genuine miracle or a deception. The Dean agreed and then requested his superior to convoke an Episcopal Commission for the investigation of the facts. Rummaging in a desk drawer, the Bishop brought forth a bundle of documents—the plans for the Commission of Investigation—expressing the hope he would never have to use them, just to avoid the possibility that they come upon, in the end, some monstrous canard and thus do immeasurable harm to the Church. The cautious conscience of Bishop Severe assumed the role of "Devil's Advocate."

The turmoil still raged around Massabielle four or five times, despite the round-the-clock doubling of the guards. The wooden fence barricading the public from the Grotto was demolished. Fines were levied upon anyone caught taking the spring water. Bernadette was apathetic to all this fuss and furor. Patiently she waited for the Lady's call, knowing full well the wall and the guards would present no serious obstacle to her will. Months passed. Dean Peyramale granted the favored one permission to make her First Holy Communion.

The sixteenth day of July, as evening shadows lengthened across the valley of the Gave, Bernadette somehow knew the Lady requested her presence at the Grotto. This time Bernadette, desiring to be alone, traversed the same route as the one taken the day of the first visitation. However, word quickly spread throughout the town. The crowd followed. She made no effort to cross the brook, but knelt on the opposite bank across from Massabielle —the same spot on which she had knelt on the eleventh day of February, now seemingly so long ago. The Grotto half-hidden by the wall of boards, the niche was barely visible above the guarded barrier.

Suddenly Bernadette saw the beautiful Lady in front of the Grotto near the bank of the river. Bernadette did not perform the usual ceremonies. Her face took on the pallor of death. She remained deeply entranced long after night had set in and the star-studded sky canopied the valley of the Gave. Finally she struggled to her feet, staggered toward her mother and collapsed. After a long period Bernadette regained consciousness but remained prone, unable to move. She was carried home to the cachot, never to return to Massabielle. The spring was not for her—the Lady had bid farewell to little Bernadette.

Doctor Dozous hospitalized the mortally exhausted child. Under the good care of the Sisters of Nevers she soon recovered. It was decided to have her live with the Sisters, sheltered from pestering strangers and their interminable curious questions.

Pride ravages the soul and defeat like a cankerous sore arrogantly demands satisfaction. The Prosecutor of Lourdes and the Prefect of the Pyrenees had suffered devastating defeat on the occasion of the phony plantation of the golden coin. Their acute dislike for little Bernadette had become a fetish that prodded them into rash action again. A psychiatrist was called upon to determine the mental condition of the child. If found deranged (and they made sure the diagnosis would be so), Bernadette would be taken into custody and kept under restraint as a public menace.

The psychiatrist appeared at the hospital. Bernadette refused to be lured into any traps. Her answers were straightforward, honest and lucid. The interrogator, in his endeavor to make a fool of her, succeeded only in making a fool of himself. Tired of the interminable questions and pin-pricking, Bernadette fled from the hospital.

Later the psychiatrist and the Imperial Prosecutor entered the cachot; they were startled to be confronted by no less a person than the Dean of Lourdes. The Doctor introduced himself as a Professor Extraordinaire of Psychiatry. The Prosecutor needed no introduction, stating that their mission

**Bernadette
in the costume
of the village.**

**Don Peyramale,
Pastor at Lourdes.**

was to place Bernadette under protective custody for observation. The Dean drew himself up to his full height and informed them that they would have to take her over his dead body. Checkmated, they withdrew. A short time later, Louise and Bernadette Soubirous, in the company of the Dean, left Lourdes by coach for Cauterets in the high mountains. Thus the persecuted little one found a safe hiding place under the protection and care of the local parish priest.

It just so happened that the Bishop of Montpellier, while taking a brief rest cure at Cauterets, made the acquaintance of Bernadette. His knowledge of the apparitions of Lourdes was only what he had gleaned from the articles in the newspapers. His opinion was similar to most of the French clergy, that extreme caution was to be observed in respect of mystical appearances of any kind. Nevertheless he asked Bernadette for an exact account of her experiences. Heretofore, such requests were acquiesced to with a mere mechanical repetition of facts. However, this time she told her story of love with great depth and fervent ecstasy. On reaching the point when the Lady requested her to visit the Grotto for fifteen consecutive days, the Bishop arose and left the room, his eyes bathed in tears.

Before returning home the good Bishop visited Lourdes and, after interrogating some trustworthy witnesses of the visions and ecstasies of Bernadette, had quite a conference with the Bishop of Tarbes. Shortly thereafter, the Dean of Lourdes was summoned to the Chancellor, where he was angrily accused by his Superior of having the entire Episcopate of France hound him. Handing the Dean an impressive scroll heavy with official seals, he ordered him to read. It was the "Ordinance of the Bishop of Lourdes Looking Toward the Appointment of a Commission for the Investigation of Those Events Which Stand in any Relationship to the Alleged Appearances in a Grotto West of Lourdes." It was quite a lengthy document. The Commission was to be composed of professors of dogmatic theology, moral and mystic theology, with an equal number of professors of medicine, chemistry, physics and geology—among the men to be convoked was the Dean of Lourdes.

But before the Commission would be commanded to assemble, the Bishop would wait until the barriers were removed and the Grotto opened (only on edict of the Emperor himself). He gave the Lady the chance of overcoming the Emperor, or of being overcome by him—now indeed the gauntlet lay at the Lady's feet.

Chapter Seven

Turmoil at Grotto—
The Emperor Acts

The smoldering embers of insurrection needed only a faint breath of righteous indignation to fan into a raging conflagration the decadent social structure of Louis Napoleon's regime. Antoine the miller, who had on two occasions carried the entranced Bernadette from the Grotto, was the winnowing cataclysmic agent. Rumor circulated that Bernadette had been kidnapped and locked in prison. Antoine made speeches inciting the laboring classes to action—hundreds laid down their tools and marched enmasse to Massabielle. The gendarmes had to draw their swords to repel the attackers who rained down stones upon the minions of the law. "The Battle of Massabielle" was only terminated when the men were given assurance that Bernadette was safe and sound. But all demanded to see her. The Dean had Louise and Bernadette return to Lourdes and took them for a carriage ride through the town. They were greeted with jubilation.

Mayor Lacade had surreptitiously sent a sample of the water taken from the spring to a renowned hydrologist for analysis. His dream of a radiant result was shattered—the report read "no therapeutic value, ordinary drinking water," composition of which corresponds exactly to that of the ' mountain springs of that region of France. "It may be used without either advantage or harm." His dream of fabulous profit from a gigantic watering place for the wealthy disappeared.

Lourdes in 1877.

The Imperial Prosecutor was having difficulties with his superiors. He was given a stinging rebuke after the tumult at the Grotto during which one of the gendarmes was painfully wounded. He decided to tighten security at the Grotto. The guards were to report all infractions of his decree, especially Article I, forbidding the taking of water from the spring. Shortly after the circumscription orders were issued, one of the police brought to the prosecutor's office a pompous lady dressed in full fashion. She had taken a bottle of springwater. Her arraignment divulged the fact that she was the wife of the former Minister of Marine. The water was taken at the request of no less a personage than her majesty, the Empress Eugenie.

The prosecutor began to see the folly of his actions in the name of duty in a topsy-turvy world. High upon a cliff overlooking the Atlantic, the summer villa at Biarritz, the Lady triumphed over the State. The third Napoleon planned the destinies of the nations of Europe, but was no match in handling the Empress Eugenie. Lou Lou, his own son, was ailing with a slight fever. The head of state was frightened; the future of the Imperial house of Corsica depended on the child's health. The Empress was distraught. With tear-filled eyes she eventually persuaded the Emperor to allow the child to drink a glass of water from Massabielle. Within twenty-four hours the child's temperature was back to normal. A grateful mother insisted that public acknowledgement of her faith in the spring and the Lady be made. After much persuasion, Napoleon III sent a telegram to the Prefect of Tarbes, "Access to the

Grotto West of Lourdes is to be immediately granted to the public." The Lady of Lourdes had found a most effective ally in Eugenie.

Baron Massy, dismayed at such an order, decided to delay its execution. To gain time he went on a tour of inspection and spent some days in Lourdes. Since the Mayor originally issued the order closing the Grotto *he* should be the one to reopen it. He refused. The Prefect then instructed the local prosecutor and the police to deal lightly with any infractions. The gendarmerie were to be removed. No more fines to be imposed. The people were suspicious and remained on the right bank opposite the Grotto.

The Emperor was furious on learning his orders were ignored. The Baron was commanded to obey instantly. Accordingly, the town crier, to the roll of drum beat, declared the Ordinance regarding the Grotto of Massabielle nullified. The workmen of Lourdes who had refused to build the barrier refused to dismantle it. The police were forced to do the job themselves, while the people observed in ominous silence. The long siege ended. The cacophonous, strident voices of atheist and nihilist that had joined forces with the State and civic authorities' envy and greed were now mute. The fools of Satan, from the gates of hell, began to look more and more like the "faun," a Roman rural mythological deity having a human body with pointed ears, horns and hind legs of a goat.

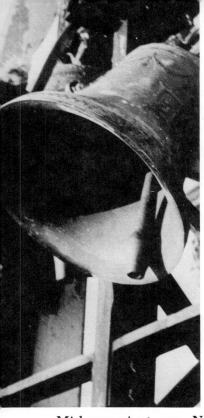

Chapter Eight

The Ecclesiastical Commission Officially Opened

Mid-morning on November 17th the deep throated peals of the bells of St. Pierre in Lourdes reverberated through the valley of the Gave, and the sun-glazed tips of the Pyrenean hills reflected the golden glory of their Creator. No official obstacle any longer gave the Bishop any right to postpone the investigation of the sacred and delicate matter of Massabielle. The "Veni Creator Spiritus" was intoned. The Commission assembled in front of the high altar was placed under the special protection of the Holy Spirit. The membership was comprised not only of professors of dogmatic, moral and mystical theology, but of an equal number of professors of medicine, chemistry, physics and geology—every instrumentality of modern, critical science was to be exhaustively employed to prove natural explanation, before the fact of supernatural interposition was to be admitted. Four years was the allotted time granted the Commission to conclude either "This Is" or "This IS NOT the finger of God."

The service of invocation concluded, the Commission began the first plenary session. Bernadette Soubirous was summoned as the first witness. Over and over she had to tell her story with numerous interruptions to confirm or correct her delineation. The other witnesses called often suffered from memory failure—not so with Bernadette. No detail, no matter how minute, had been extinguished from her mind. This fact made a powerful impression on the investigating commission who were astonished at the clarity and honesty of her replies. The investigation meticulously examined every facet of the ordinary, extraordinary and the preternatural and possibly supernatural happenings at Massabielle. Their examination of cures was tantamount to a criminal investigation.

Processions proceeded, ever increasing in numbers. The myriad flickering candles, like the fervent "Aves," all depicted the faith and devotion visibly and vocally of the people's deep love for the beautiful Lady of the Grotto. Miraculous cures increased as the inquisition continued its work, month in and month out—sifting, examining, testing and tabulating, but with no final conclusion—for time has more portent in the cognition of

First procession—1864.

truth than the most astute human intelligence. It
remained to be seen whether the miraculous cures
would continue or cease, if there would be any
diminution of devotion, and thus prove only an
evanescent popular movement of the weary
masses.

The most severe tests were applied to the
cures—only the immediacy of a lightning cure
would be accepted, such as a blind eye becoming a
seeing eye in a twinkling, or an atrophied muscle
showing living tension on the instant.

During the early period of the Commission's investigation fifteen people were instantly cured. Hundreds recovered as incomprehensibly but more slowly—tens of thousands came to Lourdes seeking new health and life. The favors of Divine Providence were granted in an unfathomable way.

In the medical examination of the cured, the most welcomed testimony was that of physicians of the non-Catholic faith or of confessed enemies of all faiths.

Amid all this stream of stirring events, Bernadette lived as though it did not concern her. Sometimes she lived at home, sometimes in the hospital. The Bishop had requested constant watch be kept over her, mainly to protect her from the curious, pestiferous public. Nearing the end of the

Pope Pius IX.

fourth year of the Commission's investigations, the most sceptical of all yielded to the overwhelming proof of the findings of the august body of the inquisition. Bishop Severe Laurence had been vanquished. In a pastoral letter he at last acknowledged the supernatural character of the visions and healings of Lourdes. He submitted his own judgment to the judgment of the Bishop of Rome, Pius IX, the "Vicar of Christ."

Permission was granted to build the chapel requested by the Lady. Within a few weeks, money for that purpose flowed in from all over the world. The donations of two million francs were composed of mostly pennies and sous from the purses of the poor. Plans were formulated to beautify the property adjacent to the Grotto. Architectural sketches of a basilica were made. Artists sculptured images

of the Lady of Lourdes. Bishop Laurence decided to expiate for his long scepticism and announced that on April 4th, when the Pyrenean countryside would be in full bloom of a new Springtime, he personally would lead the consecration procession to the Grotto. Hundreds of priests and religious of many orders were to be present at the great *Te Deum.*

On that morning, Bernadette was also to be honored, but she was overcome by the most severe attack of asthma she had suffered in years. She was unable to join the solemn ceremonies. The bells began to ring and an estimated hundred-thousand people paid grateful homage to the Immaculate Mother of God, in the valley of the Gave.

Promptly at noon the celebration came to an end. Promptly at noon Bernadette was well again. Her illness confirmed the Lady's prophecy that there would be no happy earthly day for her.

Shortly after the Church's recognition and approval of the supernatural happenings at Massabielle, the Bishop of Nevers questioned Bernadette as to her plans for the future. The renunciation of the world was most welcome—she would take the veil as one of the Sisters of Nevers. Her farewell of all her friends and family was an emotional experience. The cachot was now desolate, like a house of mourning. Her sorrow was not the pain of parting, but more one of pity for her family—a pity that would never know consolation.

Bernadette, now Sister Marie-Bernard.

Before leaving Lourdes her carriage stopped for a visit at the Grotto. She blessed herself and in anguish slowly turned and walked away. The shrine of miraculous blessings for countless millions till the end of time was not for her. As a bride of Christ, the favorite child of the Immaculate Queen of Heaven spent the remainder of her life in one of the noblest monastic establishments of all France, and blossomed into the spiritual perfection striven for by all good religious.

The Holy Cross infirmary where Bernadette died. *(Her bed is designated by the cross.)*

The tomb of Bernadette.

God granted her the grace of the imitation of Christ. Her terminal illness was a malignancy that destroyed the bone tissue in her legs and shoulders. Two years of excruciating martyrdom and Bernadette could walk no more. When it was suggested she be taken to Lourdes, she declined, saying "the Spring was not for her."

The doctor informed Mother Superior that the death of Sister Marie Bernarde was imminent. The Bishops of Tarbes and Nevers, with their emissaries, sundry clerics and learned theologians, formed a Commission to witness a final confirmation of the truth of testimony offered by Bernadette to the Commission of 1858.

In spite of her great pain, she retold her story of the beautiful Lady in the lilting, clear voice of her childhood. "I did see her; I did see her"—it was on a Thursday, the 11th of February that Bernadette first saw the beautiful Lady. On Thursday of Holy Week, 16th of April, 1879, at thirty-five years of age, Bernadette joined the beautiful Lady in the kingdom of her divine Son.

The tomb of the Saint.

**Pope
Pius XI.**

On December 8th, 1933, the Feast of the Immaculate Conception, the Vicar of Christ, Pius XI, amid the splendors of the Basilica of St. Peter in Rome declared: "Blessed Marie Bernarde Soubirous is a saint." The deep thunder of the chimes of St. Peter's re-echoed the joyous message to the world. Official records of the Church name her St. Mary Bernarde, but to the faithful, lovingly she will always be St. Bernadette—born of the union of François and Louise Soubirous, January 7, 1844.

Chapter Nine

Lourdes, the Pain Capital of the World

In the early days of the shrine, demonic denizens of stygian darkness, clothed in the garb of doubters, mockers and haters created a tumult, in a vain effort to veil the miraculous eternal truths of Lourdes from the eyes of the world. They pictured Lourdes as the "Mecca of crackpots to be cured of imaginary diseases"—"no doctor worth his salt would have put an ounce of credence in Lourdes" —"Lourdes was nothing more than an exploitation of human stupidity."

The fury and turmoil has increased through the years, yet thousands of pilgrims daily drink of the water and bathe in the spring of miracles. A change has taken place in the attitude of the medical profession concerning the cures at Lourdes. They use the term "medically inexplicable"— never "miracle." The well-respected work of the Medical Bureau at Lourdes is largely responsible for this change. The records show more than twenty-five hundred miracles up to 1917. Today the Church stands on its collective head to avoid any possible misuse of the term "miracle." Now only one or two are verified yearly by the Bureau —no illness which could possibly be classed as psychosomatic would even be studied. This is regrettable, for the "crying need of our day is the miracle that cures the disordered mind, the emotionally disturbed"—"these are the very cures to claim authentic—thousands of such disturbed people leave Lourdes each year, at *peace.*"

Those who know Lourdes well, claim that everyone who comes to the Shrine is cured, even those who do not receive a physical healing, for they leave joyful, keenly aware of God's love for them. Yearly hundreds of cures are never reported or recorded.

No case is studied by the Medical Bureau unless some organic change has occurred. A patient must have a certificate from his doctor, stating his disease, present condition, and its progress at the time he left home. If he believes himself cured, he is examined, scientifically X-rayed, and laboratory tests as needed are taken. The miraculee must then go home and be re-examined by his own

doctor who must in turn certify his findings to the Medical Bureau at Lourdes. Indubitably the chronicle of many true healings comes to an end right here, because of the reticence of medical men to admit to anything so unscientific as a miracle.

If the doctor has cooperated, the miraculee must return one year later to Lourdes. His case is gone over and he is subjected to cross-questioning similar to a criminal investigation. If the findings are that a genuine cure has taken place, the case is sent to the Medical Commission in Paris, to be intensively examined. The duty of the International Medical Commission of Lourdes is not to declare a miracle, but to declare or fail to declare "no natural or scientific explanation for this cure." If such a declaration is forthcoming, it is recommended to the miraculee's local ordinary that a canonical commission be appointed to investigate the cure. If after two years the cure is found to be maintained, the theologians, not the doctors, declare it is a miracle. "Hic est digitus Dei." So severe is the judgment of the theologians that little more than fifty percent of the cures submitted are declared miraculous.

About the turn of the century a great hubbub arose, charging that the water of Lourdes was so polluted by the many sick and suppurating bodies bathed in it, that it was a health hazard and the Shrine definitely should be closed—this, despite the fact that no invalid brought to Lourdes had ever returned home any worse for having been immersed. More than three thousand doctors testified to the invaluable service rendered to the sick by Lourdes in cases where medical science had no hope to offer.

Realizing the truth of the foulness of the waters, the Medical Bureau doctors had a series of tests made in 1934 and 1935—two samples of the water were taken after the last bath where the men's wounds were bathed. One sample was sent to a laboratory in Anvers; the other to the Provincial Laboratory of Bacteriological Analysis of the province of Grand, in Belgium. Neither laboratory knew the source of the water—both reported that "the water contained many varieties of deadly microbes, but did absolutely no harm to the guinea pigs used in the test." Six months later the animals

were still alive and healthy. The same tests were run with water taken from the Seine River and another unknown source containing much the same microorganisms as in the Lourdes water. "All the animals developed high fever, and two out of three died."

As an act of faith many bathers scoop up a glass of water from the baths and drink it down. Your author has participated in this profession of faith on many occasions with no mal-effects. Also an application of this same spring water to a cancerous growth located in the temple area of his face affected an instantaneous cure. Every trace of the malignant growth instantly vanished. The Lourdes water used was some he had procured on a visit to the Shrine more than a year previously.

Chapter Ten

A Pilgrimage to Lourdes Via the White Train

For twenty-two years, the legendary "White Train" has wended its way from Rome to Lourdes —gathering up at every stop the blind, the lame, the deaf and the handicapped. Hundreds gather as the wheelchairs, litter cases and others board the train. They do not just stand and watch: they hand up homemade bread, homegrown vegetables, wine they made themselves, flowers grown in their own gardens. They are accompanying the train in spirit, singing, praying and saying with their gifts of themselves, "Immaculate Mother of God—Help our sick Priests."

Happily Americans were privileged to be invited to join the White Train Pilgrimage. A goodly number of Americans, including your author, joined this spiritual journey.

The Pilgrimage officially started with a special audience with our Holy Father, Pope Paul VI, at Castel Gandolfo. John Cardinal Wright and Bishop Maloney accompanied us as we traveled along the Italian Riviera through the Pyrenean hills and on to our Lady's Shrine.

Our stay at Lourdes was indeed an unforgettable spiritual experience. Holy Mass was daily concelebrated for the pilgrims by Cardinal Wright, Bishop Maloney and the Priests. A retreat for the clergy was conducted by the inimitable, dynamic, beloved Cardinal Wright.

A special radio broadcast to Rome and Pope Paul VI from the Grotto of our Lady of Lourdes featured a welcome address by the Bishop of Lourdes, and a response by Bishop Maloney of Wichita, Kansas. Monsignor Novarese conducted the beautiful chorale of sonorous Italian priest voices. The "Domain" of Lourdes in the Pyrenean valley of the Gave reverberated with the "Aves" of the Rosary and the "Salve Regina." That must have brought joy to the heart of the Vicar of Christ, a smile to the lips of Christ's Holy Mother, and peace to the thousands of her children pouring forth their great faith, fervent hope and tremendous love at her Shrine. If indeed there were sceptics in that day's audience, their doubts surely must have dissolved in the light of this demonstration that "God is not dead."

Cardinal Wright concelebrated Holy Mass with more than five hundred priests in the Pius X Basilica on the occasion of the Twenty-Fifth Anniversary of his consecration as Bishop—tens of thousands received Holy Communion in the prescribed manner from the hands of the Priests.

Thousands marching in the procession with the Blessed Sacrament and the blessing of the sick, bathing at the spring and drinking of the water in fulfillment of our Blessed Lady's request. The humble joy of receiving the sacrament of Penance; the torturous stations of the Cross; the beautiful, spectacular candlelight procession in the cool of the early darkness of the Pyrenean night—all these unforgettable, beautiful experiences were most aptly summed up by one of the pilgrims when she said, "I have never been happier in my life. I could spend the rest of it here. This is like a bit of heaven on earth."

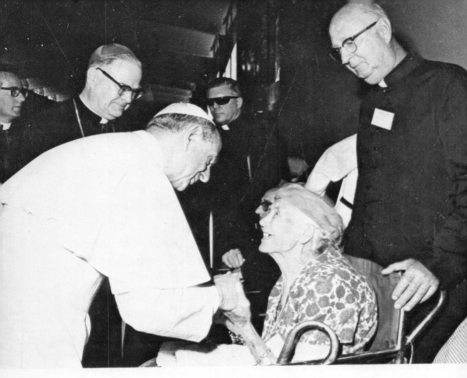

Tired but happy, the pilgrims returned to America. None with headline-making miracles to report—but all with an inner feeling of peace and acceptance of the Cross of Pain God had placed upon them, which sometimes is the greatest miracle of all.

Although faceless horsemen from Hades' garrison—Doubt, Mockery and Hate—still ride roughshod o'er the pathways of time, Mary's legions continue to march undaunted to Lourdes in ever-increasing numbers—seeking relief from pain, hoping and praying for the miraculous cure, cognizant of the fact that Our Lady's appearances proved the universe held more than this mere mortal misery. They were *not*—are *not*—nor ever shall be disappointed.

Dear God, see how they love Your Holy Mother, and each other! Marching with hope in their hearts, a smile on their faces abnegating the raging pain of a disease-racked body, prayers of penance and petition on their lips, their multitudinous voices lilting in song—"Ave, Ave, Ave, Maria."

"Oh Holy Virgin in the midst of Thy days of glory, forget not the sorrows of this earth. Cast Thy glance upon those who are surrounded with difficulties, whose lips tremble with the bitterness of life. Have pity on those who love one another and are separated; have pity on the loneliness of our hearts, on the weakness of our faith, on the objects of our love. Have pity on those who weep, and those who pray; give hope to all, give peace to all, and give to us the joy of one day seeing Thee in Heaven.
                                                                    Amen."

My apology for being so presumptuous as to attempt to relate "The Massabielle Saga," knowing full well that to do it justice would take words coined of purest spun gold, lovingly uttered in dulcet tones by the tongue of one of God's Archangels.

However, "That praise of our Blessed Lady shall ne'er depart from the lips of Men," I humbly offer with love this Saga to Mary, my Mother.

                                                        Rev. James H. Klein

Daughters of St. Paul

IN MASSACHUSETTS
50 St. Paul's Ave. Jamaica Plain, Boston, MA 02130;
617-522-8911; 617-522-0875;
172 Tremont Street, Boston, MA 02111; **617-426-5464;
617-426-4230**
IN NEW YORK
78 Fort Place, Staten Island, NY 10301; **212-447-5071**
59 East 43rd Street, New York, NY 10017; **212-986-7580**

625 East 187th Street, Bronx, NY 10458; **212-584-0440**
525 Main Street, Buffalo, NY 14203; **716-847-6044**
IN NEW JERSEY
Hudson Mall — Route 440 and Communipaw Ave.,
Jersey City, NJ 07304; **201-433-7740**
IN CONNECTICUT
202 Fairfield Ave., Bridgeport, CT 06604; **203-335-9913**
IN OHIO
2105 Ontario St. (at Prospect Ave.), Cleveland, OH 44115; **216-621-9427**
25 E. Eighth Street, Cincinnati, OH 45202; **513-721-4838**
IN PENNSYLVANIA
1719 Chestnut Street, Philadelphia, PA 19103; **215-568-2638**
IN FLORIDA
2700 Biscayne Blvd., Miami, FL 33137; **305-573-1618**
IN LOUISIANA
4403 Veterans Memorial Blvd., Metairie, LA 70002; **504-887-7631;
504-887-0113**
1800 South Acadian Thruway, P.O. Box 2028, Baton Rouge, LA 70821
504-343-4057; 504-343-3814
IN MISSOURI
1001 Pine Street (at North 10th), St. Louis, MO 63101; **314-621-0346;
314-231-1034**
IN ILLINOIS
172 North Michigan Ave., Chicago, IL 60601; **312-346-4228;
312-346-3240**
IN TEXAS
114 Main Plaza, San Antonio, TX 78205; **512-224-8101**
IN CALIFORNIA
1570 Fifth Avenue, San Diego, CA 92101; **714-232-1442**
46 Geary Street, San Francisco, CA 94108; **415-781-5180**
IN HAWAII
1143 Bishop Street, Honolulu, HI 96813; **808-521-2731**
IN ALASKA
750 West 5th Avenue, Anchorage AK 99501; **907-272-8183**
IN CANADA
3022 Dufferin Street, Toronto 395, Ontario, Canada
IN ENGLAND
128, Notting Hill Gate, London W11 3QG, England
133 Corporation Street, Birmingham B4 6PH, England
5A-7 Royal Exchange Square, Glasgow G1 3AH, England
82 Bold Street, Liverpool L1 4HR, England
IN AUSTRALIA
58 Abbotsford Rd., Homebush, N.S.W., Sydney 2140, Australia